modern readers — stage 4

In the Dark

Eduardo Amos
Elisabeth Prescher
Ernesto Pasqualin

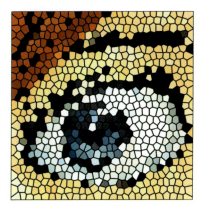

Os autores agradecem a Lucília Gioradno e Ananda Giordano Perez pelas valiosas informações prestadas.

Richmond

© EDUARDO AMOS, ELISABETH PRESCHER, ERNESTO PASQUALIN, 2004

Diretoria: *Paul Berry*
Gerência editorial: *Sandra Possas*
Coordenação de revisão: *Estevam Vieira Lédo Jr.*
Coordenação de produção gráfica: *André Monteiro, Maria de Lourdes Rodrigues*
Coordenação de produção industrial: *Wilson Troque*

Projeto editorial: *Véra Regina A. Maselli, Kylie Mackin*

Assistência editorial: *Gabriela Peixoto Vilanova*
Revisão: *Denise Ceron*
Projeto gráfico de miolo e capa: *Ricardo Van Steen Comunicações e Propaganda Ltda./Oliver Fuchs*
Edição de arte: *Christiane Borin*
Ilustrações de miolo e capa: *Rogério Borges*
Diagramação: *EXATA Editoração*
Pré-impressão: *Hélio P. de Souza Filho, Marcio H. Kamoto*
Impressão e acabamento: Gráfica Elyon
Lote: 749362

Dados Internacionais de Catalogação na Publicação (CIP)
(Câmara Brasileira do Livro, SP, Brasil)

Amos, Eduardo
　　In the dark / Eduardo Amos, Elisabeth Prescher, Ernesto Pasqualin ; (ilustrações Rogério Borges). — São Paulo : Moderna, 2003. — (Modern Readers ; stage 4)

　　1. Inglês (Ensino fundamental) I. Prescher, Elisabeth. II. Pasqualin, Ernesto. III. Borges, Rogério. IV. Título. V. Série.

03-3370　　　　　　　　　　　　　　　　　　CDD-372.652

Índices para catálogo sistemático:
1. Inglês : Ensino fundamental　372.652

ISBN 85-16-03724-X

Reprodução proibida. Art. 184 do Código Penal e Lei 9.610 de 19 de fevereiro de 1998.

Todos os direitos reservados.

RICHMOND
SANTILLANA EDUCAÇÃO LTDA.
Rua Padre Adelino, 758, 3º andar – Belenzinho
São Paulo – SP – Brasil – CEP 03303-904
www.richmond.com.br
2022

Impresso no Brasil

Chapter 1

I first heard about Ananda six or seven years ago. At that time, Ananda's mother told me it was difficult to find an appropriate school for her. The years passed and I forgot about Ananda.

This year, however, her mother contacted me again. Ananda needed one of my English books in braille.

But who is Ananda?

She is a regular sixteen-year-old girl. She has friends and she goes to school and parties. She also likes studying English and playing the keyboard and the drums. The only difference is that Ananda is visually-impaired.

What I am going to tell you happened last year, when Ananda was fifteen. It is an amazing story.

"Ananda, where are you?"

"In my bedroom! I'm doing my homework," Ananda answered Lucia Marcondes, her mother.

"Hi, sweetheart! Have you finished?" asked Mrs Marcondes, approaching Ananda.

"Yes, Mom. Can you print this out for me? It's for my History class tomorrow."

Ananda did her homework on the computer, and a special device printed everything out in braille.

"Dani and Jessica are coming over later. We are going to study."

"Who's Jessica?" asked Mrs Marcondes.

She's Dani's friend. Now she's my friend, too," answered Ananda. "Can they stay for dinner and sleep here tonight?"

"Sure!" said Mrs Marcondes.

Ananda didn't have many friends where she lived. People don't approach the blind very easily. Her few friends were her classmates at school. Dani was her best friend and they did everything together. Jessica was a new friend.

That afternoon, the girls were talking in Ananda's bedroom.

"I don't get it, Ananda," said Jessica. "How do you find your things, your clothes, your shoes? Isn't it difficult?"

"Not at all," Ananda answered, smiling at her new friend. "This is my closet. Look! Mom labeled everything in braille; white T-shirts, dark T-shirts, jeans, etc.... But sometimes I mix up my tennis shoes!"

"Can your mother read braille?" asked Jessica.

"Yes, she can. She had to help me when I was little. Now I can read quite fluently."

"Don't you trip over things?" Jessica asked.

"No. Ooops!" cried Ananda falling over a chair that Jessica had left in the way. "Not if everything is in the right place."

"Oh, I'm sorry, Ananda," Jessica said.

When Mrs Marcondes called the girls for dinner, they had been talking for a long time. Jessica was surprised to learn about Ananda's life. She had never thought that a blind person could play musical instruments, read, study, and move around the house so well.

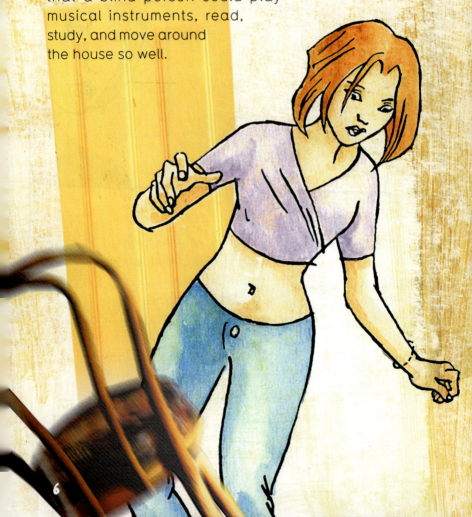

"Well, girls, this is what we have for dinner," said Mrs Marcondes. "... rice, vegetables, chicken, and potatoes. Do you want me to make up your plate, Ananda?"

"Yes, Mom. I'm starving."

"Here you are!" said Mrs Marcondes. "Rice at 12 o'clock, vegetables at 3 o'clock, chicken at 6 o'clock, and potatoes at 9 o'clock." Mrs Marcondes always described the position of the food on the plate to help Ananda.

"I'm glad I came over to your place today, Ananda," said Jessica. "I got to know you better."

Chapter 2

When Mrs Marcondes left the girls at school the next day, they went in different directions.

"I have to talk to the Geography teacher," said Dani.

"Me too," Jessica added.

"Well, I'm going to English class," Ananda said. "See you later!"

Ananda walked around the school by herself. It wasn't a problem for her. She knew the school quite well. She walked down the hall, crossed the yard, passed in front of the snack bar, and turned left.

She was thinking about her English lesson. She liked English a lot. She could read, write, and speak well, but she didn't like Listening Comprehension exercises which involved using pictures. Someone had to describe the pictures to her before she could do the activities.

Ananda was so deep in thought that she didn't hear the footsteps. They were approaching fast. Suddenly...

... a boy collided into her.

Ananda fell onto the floor. Her English books flew all over the place.

"Oh, sorry," the boy said. "I was looking for the lab and I didn't see you. I'm really sorry. Are you OK?"

Tiago was a new student and he didn't know his way around the school yet.

"Sure. I'm all right. I can take you to the lab," Ananda said.

"But," Tiago said, "you can't see, can you?"

"No. I'm blind, but I can take you anywhere in the school."

As they walked to the lab, Tiago was feeling embarrassed. He told Ananda that this was the first time he had met a blind person. He didn't know what to do.

"Well, thanks a lot," he said when they got to the lab. "It was great getting to know you."

Chapter 3

Lucia Marcondes answered the phone. It was her mother.
"Hi, Mom."
"Is everyone all right?" asked Mrs Cunha. "How's Ananda doing?"
"Oh, she's fine. She is very happy that she has made a new friend at school. His name is Tiago. He came over the other day and he is a nice kid."
"That's good to hear, Lucia. Ananda has so few friends. I often worry about that. People seem to be afraid of the visually-impaired."
"I don't think so, Mom. I think that people just don't know what to do around the blind."
"Anyway, it doesn't matter. The thing is that Ananda needs more friends. That's why I'm calling you."
"What do you mean?"
"There is a holiday at the end of the month. Why don't you invite some of Ananda's classmates over here? The house is big. There is the lake and the beach. The kids will have fun."
"I don't know, Mom. I have to talk to Claudio. Perhaps she is too young."
"Come on, Lucia! Ananda is fifteen. She needs company of her own age. Talk to Claudio and call me back."

At first, Mrs Marcondes didn't like the idea. Ananda was quite independent in places she knew well like her grandparents' house. She had been to their place on the lake many times. But she had never been there with her friends. Many people around her could be risky.

But Ananda was so excited at the idea that her mother finally gave in. The Marcondes invited some of Ananda's school friends. Everything was carefully planned. The great day arrived at last.

Chapter 4

Ananda's grandparents had a lovely house by a lake. It had a porch, a large dining room with a fireplace, and bedrooms for everybody. The kids liked the house and the mountains around it.

Ananda's family was happy and so were the kids. They had three days ahead of them, and the weather was perfect.

Mrs Marcondes decided it was time to give them some basic instructions:

"Remember, kids. Ananda can't see. Just tell her where things are. Tell her where you are. Use words like 'right, left, in front of' and don't leave things in her way. She knows this place. If you do what I say, Ananda won't have any problems."

The kids found the instructions easy to follow and soon everyone was getting along well. They talked, laughed, swam and even played ball.

The adults were on the porch watching them.

"They are having a good time, Lucia. Why don't you relax?"

"You're right, Mom. They are getting along well and they seem to be having a good time. It was a great idea to invite the other kids."

Everything was going on so well that, at the end of the day, when the kids said that they wanted to camp on the beach, nobody objected. Ananda and her friends spent the rest of the evening putting up tents and making a fire. When everything was ready, they sat around the fire to talk.

"This is a beautiful place," said Tatiana.

"I never thought you could help us set up camp, Ananda. But you did!" said Gabriel.

"Well," replied Ananda. "It's all a question of training your memory. I've had lots of practice."

"What is difficult for you to do?" asked Jessica.

"You won't believe this, but I have a hard time combing my hair and putting toothpaste on my toothbrush!"

They talked till late that night. By the time they fell asleep, everyone felt closer to Ananda.

Very early the next morning, Lucia woke the kids up. She was very upset.

"What's wrong?" Ananda asked.

"Grandma fainted in the kitchen. I have to get her to a hospital," Lucia answered.

"Where is Dad?" Ananda asked.

"He and Grandpa went out fishing. They left very early. Now, everybody listen to me! Go inside and have some breakfast. If I'm not back by lunchtime, fix some sandwiches. Ananda knows where everything is. Please, stay inside or on the beach and don't go far from the house. I'll be back as soon as I can."

The kids were worried and upset, and spent the morning in the house. But by lunchtime, they were getting restless.

"Let's have a picnic!" suggested Fabiana.

"We can't go far," Dani warned.

"You guys go. I'll stay here," said Ananda.

Chapter 5

"I can see a great place," Gabriel said. "It isn't very far away, Ananda. If we walk along the lake, it will be easy for you."

"Come on, Ananda!" Jessica pleaded. "We'll guide you. It's going to be fun."

Ananda wasn't happy about the idea, but she didn't want to disappoint her new friends.

"Okay, I'll come too. Let's make some sandwiches."

The kids prepared everything they needed. Gabriel insisted on taking the binoculars and a flashlight.

They walked along the lake and after one hour they arrived at the place Gabriel had seen from the house.

"Isn't this a cool place? Look at that waterfall!" he said.

"Well, I'm starving! Let's eat!" said Caio. "Then we can go to the waterfall."

They were still eating when Gabriel shouted.
"Look! Over there behind the waterfall. Can you see it?"
The kids looked in the direction Gabriel was pointing to.
"What is it?" Ananda asked.

They told her there was an entrance to a cave behind the waterfall. They decided to explore it.

Gabriel was the first inside. He was holding the flashlight.

Ananda was the last. She had one hand on Tiago's shoulder.

Ananda touched the wall with the back of her other hand.

The kids described what they saw to Ananda.

The cave got narrower and there were many tunnels.

Ananda was afraid. She wanted to go back.

But they heard the sound of water...

... and convinced Ananda to go on.

"The water is to our left," said Ananda.

At the end of the tunnel, there was a big clearing.

19

"Wow! Look down there!" shouted Tatiana.
"What is it?" asked Ananda.
"A big lake," Dani replied. "I think there's a river, too."
"Look at the stalactites and stalagmites!" added Caio. "They are incredible."
"Listen! Listen to the echo!" exclaimed Fabiana.

"Do you think we can go down?" asked Jessica.
"Sure we can. Let's go!" cried Gabriel enthusiastically.
The kids were on their way down when Ananda stopped.
"Wait!" she said. "There's something wrong. The ground is shaking! Come back!"

"What are we going to do now?" cried Fabiana.

"You aren't too far down," Ananda said. "You aren't very far away from me."

"We have to climb back up," said Caio.

"Up where?" Dani asked. "In which direction?"

"We can't follow the sound of Ananda's voice because of the echo here in the cave," said Tiago in a frightened voice.

"Listen to me!" Ananda shouted. "I have a match with me. I'll try to light it. I don't know if I can, but I'll try. Then you'll see where I am."

"Ready?" she asked and lit the match.

One after the other, the kids climbed up. First the boys, then the girls. It was very hard to move in the dark. They were frightened and hurt. They couldn't see where to put their hands. But they finally climbed back to where Ananda was.

"Now what?" asked Gabriel. "What are we going to do? I can't see a thing."

"We'll never find our way out!" cried Jessica, losing control.

Tatiana was in shock and started crying. "We are going to die in this cave."

"Ananda," Tiago said. "You have to guide us out of here. You are our only chance. Do you think you can find the way out?"

"I don't know," she answered. "I can try."

"I can't move," Tatiana cried. "I can't move."

"Listen, everybody!" said Dani. "We have to get out of here. I know that Ananda can guide us out. Tell us what to do, Ananda."

"Stay in line," she said firmly. "I'll go first. Keep one hand on the wall and the other on the shoulder of the person in front of you. I'll try to remember the way back."

The kids were terrified, but followed the instructions and began their difficult journey back. They were all silent, following Ananda's directions.

"There's a tunnel on the left. Don't go into it."

"Ouch! I bumped my head on something. Watch out!"

Ananda continued on slowly. Sometimes she went in the wrong direction, but she had her other senses to help her.

"Listen!" she said. "Can't you hear the waterfall? Can't you feel the wind? We aren't very far away now. Can you see anything?"

"No," Dani answered. "It's still dark. Go on, Ananda."

And so they went on. After walking for a while, Tiago shouted, "Look! Light!"

They were so happy that they screamed and shouted.

"We did it! We are safe!" cried Tatiana.
"Because of you, Ananda. You're great!" said Gabriel.
They all gathered around Ananda and kissed and hugged her.

Many people think that blind people can't do anything by themselves. But it isn't true. Special education and training programs can help them overcome obstacles in their daily lives. They can be successful in their professions, and help people like you and me.

TIPS FOR RELATING TO THE VISUALLY-IMPAIRED

(1) You can use words like "blind, look, see," when talking to a blind person. He/she won't be offended.
(2) Use words like "left, right, behind" when giving directions. Don't point to things. Don't say "here, there."
(3) Say who you are when you arrive, and tell the person when you are leaving.
(4) Don't leave objects in the way, or doors half-open.
(5) Don't pull or push the person; simply touch him/her and offer your arm.
(6) Don't put a tray with glasses in front of the person; put a glass right in his/her hand.
(7) Prepare the person's plate and describe it to him/her.
(8) Tell the person if there is any problem with his/her hair, shoes, or clothes.
(9) Touch the person to let him/her know that you are talking to him/her.

(Adapted from "A Cegueira Trocada em Miúdos",
Helena Flávia de Rezende Melo, Univ. Est. de Campinas, 1988.)

KEY WORDS

The meaning of each word corresponds to its use in the context of the story (see page number 00)

amazing (3) incrível
anyway (10) de qualquer maneira
anywhere (9) qualquer lugar
approach, approaching (4) aproximar
blind (9) cego
bump, bumped (26) bater
camp (14) acampar
cave (17) caverna
classmate (5) colega de classe
clearing (19) espaço aberto
climb (24) subir
closet (5) armário
collapse, collapsed (22) desmoronar
comb, combing (14) pentear
come over, came over (10) vir à casa de alguém
cool (16) legal
cross, crossed (8) cruzar
daily (28) diário
drums (3) tambores
embarrassed (9) envergonhado
everyone (10) todos
everything (15) tudo
faint, fainted (15) desmaiar
fall, fell (9) cair
fall asleep, fell asleep (14) adormecer

feel, feeling (9) sentir
find (3) encontrar
fireplace (12) lareira
fix (15) fazer comida
flashlight (16) lanterna
fly, flew (9) voar
footsteps (9) passos
forget, forgot (3) esquecer
gather, gathered (27) juntar
get to know, got to know (7) conhecer melhor
get along, getting along (13) se dar bem
give in, gave in (11) concordar
glad (7) contente
ground (21) chão
guys (15) pessoal
half-open (28) entreaberta
hall (8) corredor
hear, heard (3) ouvir
hug, hugged (27) abraçar
hurt (25) machucado
hurt, hurts (23) doer
in line (25) em fila
in shock (25) em choque
invite… over (10) convidar (alguém) para (sua) casa
keep (25) manter
keyboard (3) teclado
lab (9) laboratório

label, labeled (5) etiquetar
leave, left (6) deixar
light (27) luz
light, lit (24) acender
lose control, losing control (25) perder o controle
lose, lost (23) perder
make a fire, making a fire (14) fazer uma fogueira
make up (7) preparar
match (24) fósforo
meet, met (9) conhecer
mix up (5) misturar
narrower (18) mais estreito
overcome (28) superar
plead, pleaded (16) apelar
porch (12) varanda
print (4) imprimir
put up, putting up (14) armar
risky (11) arriscado
restless (15) inquieto
rock floor (22) chão de pedra
rumbling (22) barulho alto
safe (23) seguro
scream, screamed (27) gritar
seem (10) parecer
sense (26) sentido
shake, shaking (21) tremer
shoulder (18) ombro
snack bar (8) lanchonete
sound (19) som
spend, spent (14) passar
starving (7) morrendo de fome
successful (28) bem-sucedido
sweetheart (4) querida
terrified (26) aterrorizado
themselves (28) eles mesmos
tip (28) dica

toothbrush (14) escova de dentes
toothpaste (14) pasta de dentes
touch, touched (18) tocar
train, training (14) praticar
tray (28) bandeja
trip over (6) esbarrar
upset (15) chateado
visually-impaired (3) deficiente visual
wake, woke up (15) acordar
waterfall (16) cachoeira
wind (26) vento
worried (15) preocupado
yard (8) pátio

Expressions

All of a sudden... (22) De repente
deep in thought (9) concentrado
have a hard time (14) achar difícil
I don't get it (5) Eu não consigo entender
in (someone's) way (12) no caminho (de alguém)
in the way (6) no meio do caminho
it doesn't matter (10) não importa
It's all a question of... (14) É só uma questão de...
Not at all (5) Nem um pouco
set up camp (14) montar acampamento
That's good to hear (10) É bom saber
The thing is... (10) O fato é...
Watch out! (26) Cuidado!

Before Reading

1. Place your fingers on the title of the book. It's written in a special kind of writing system. Do you know what it's called?

While Reading

Chapter One

2. Answer these questions:
   a) How does Ananda find her clothes, shoes and other things?
   b) How does Mrs Marcondes describe the food on Ananda's plate? Why?
   c) Jessica was surprised about some things in Ananda's life. Which things?

Chapter Two

3. In this chapter, Ananda describes some things which she <u>can</u> do at school and some things which <u>are difficult</u> for her. What are these things?

   Ananda can _____

   It is difficult for Ananda to _____

   _____

4. At the end of the chapter, Ananda helps Tiago. What does he learn from her?

Chapter Three

5. Correct these sentences:
   a) Ananda had never been to her grandparents' house on the lake.
   b) Ananda was quite independent in places she didn't know well.
   c) Mrs Marcondes thinks that many people around Ananda could be fun.

Chapter Four

6. Make a list of the instructions that Mrs Marcondes gives the kids about Ananda.
   Example: Tell her where things are.
   a) _____
   b) _____
   c) _____

Chapter 5

7. What happened in the cave?

8. How did Ananda help the other kids?

9. Read the "Tips for Relating to the Visually-Impaired" on page 28. Which 3 surprise you most? Talk to a friend.

After Reading (Optional Activities)

10. Find out about associations for the visually-impaired in your town/city/neighborhood. What programs do they have? Who frequents them?

11. What things could you do at your school to make it easier for a blind person studying there? Think about things like:
    — classrooms and physical installations
    — help with different subjects
    — homework

12. Find out about associations and groups in your neighborhood for any or all of the following groups:
    — the visually-impaired
    — the hearing-impaired
    — the physically disabled

    Visit one of these associations and find out about the members' special skills, abilities and everyday difficulties.